Paul Revere

Teri L. Tilwick

Boston, Massachusetts
Chandler, Arizona
Glenview, Illinois
Upper Saddle River, New Jersey

Illustrations

Opener, 1, 3, 4, 5, 8, 9, 10, 11, 14, 15 Timothy Jones.

Photographs

Every effort has been made to secure permission and provide appropriate credit for photographic material. The publisher deeply regrets any omission and pledges to correct errors called to its attention in subsequent editions.

Unless otherwise acknowledged, all photographs are the property of Pearson Education, Inc.

Photo locators denoted as follows: Top (T), Center (C), Bottom (B), Left (L), Right (R), Background (Bkgd)

2 Library of Congress; 6 Library of Congress; 7 Library of Congress; 12 Courtesy National Archives of the United States; 13 Library of Congress.

ISBN-13: 978-0-328-67590-6
ISBN-10: 0-328-67590-3

4 5 6 V0FL 16 15 14 13

Paul Revere was an American hero.

He helped our country win its freedom long ago.

Revere was born in Boston in 1735.

His father made things from silver.

His father died.

Now Revere ran the silver shop.

Revere got married and had a family.

He worked hard.

Great Britain ruled the colonies.

Many Americans did not like this.

They were called **Patriots**.

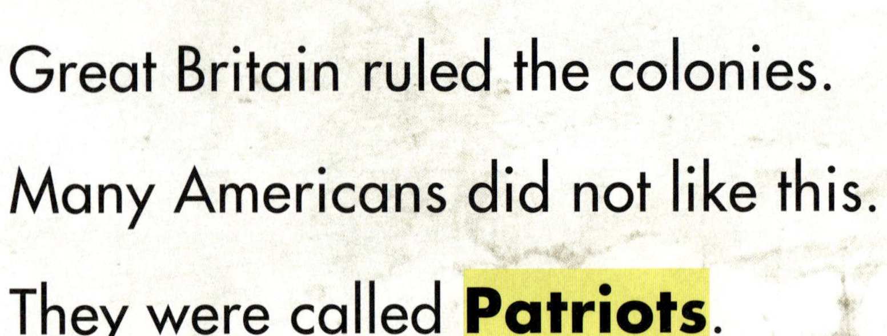

Britain made Americans pay **taxes**.

This made the Patriots mad.

They thought the taxes were not fair.

They threw British tea into the water.

Revere took messages to other Patriots.

He rode fast and far.

The messages told the Patriots to fight.

Revere became a **spy**.

He learned Britain's war plans.

The British army was about to attack!

He asked friends to warn people.

One lamp in the tower meant they were coming by land.

Two lamps meant by water.

Two lanterns shone that night.

The British were coming by boat!

Revere rode his horse.

He woke up Patriots and warned them.

Soldiers are coming!

Then a loud shot rang out.

The war for **independence** began.

The colonies finally won the war.

The United States was a free country.

Revere printed money for the new country.

Revere had a long and good life.

He was a great American Patriot.

Glossary

independence freedom

Patriots colonists who wanted independence from Britain

spy a person who finds out secrets

taxes money that people pay to a government